101 Fantastic Facts about Walt Disney World

Interesting facts, secrets, and urban legends about the world's most popular theme parks

By: Adam Wilk

TABLE OF CONTENTS

Introduction   5

Chapter 1 – Magic Kingdom   9

Chapter 2 – Epcot Future World   23

Chapter 3 – Epcot World Showcase   37

Chapter 4 – Hollywood Studios   45

Chapter 5 – Animal Kingdom   55

Before You Go _____64

The Complete Disney Travel Collection _____66

INTRODUCTION

Walt Disney World is the happiest place on Earth. You've heard it mentioned many times in many different places. If you've read any other Disney guidebooks on the market, you've certainly seen it mentioned at least a time or two in each book.

The Happiest Place on Earth

Since the opening of Magic Kingdom way back in 1971, Walt Disney World has grown into an entertainment mecca unmatched by any other theme park or entertainment complex in the world. As Disney World expanded from a single park with a few nearby resorts and restaurants to the four major theme parks, two waterparks, well over 100 restaurants, nearly 30 resorts, the Disney Springs (formerly known as Downtown Disney) shopping and entertainment district, and more, Disney has continued to provide impeccable customer service and an unparalleled guest experience. From the time you enter the first park on the first day of your stay, to the time you return home, exhausted from your adventures, you'll realize that there is no other vacation like a Disney vacation.

Walt Disney World is also home to a grand history and an abundance of mystery too. Throughout its nearly 50 year history, Disney World has changed with the times and expanded to meet the ever increasing customer demand. Over the years many old-time favorites have given way to new attractions, and many legends have grown from the history in and around the parks. That's where this book comes in.

...it was all started by a Mouse

While you'll find many great Disney travel guides in the marketplace, including several listed at the beginning of this book, you won't find a Disney book quite like this one anywhere. Rather than being a Disney vacation planner or guide to the parks, this book (as indicated in the title) covers 101 interesting and unusual facts about Walt Disney World- things that you probably didn't know (unless you've spent countless hours scouring the Internet to research them like I did) but items that you'll find very useful and interesting- at least I hope so!

If you're planning a Disney vacation, if you've just returned home and didn't quite get enough of Disney during your stay, or even if you just have a passing interest or curiosity about the history of Walt Disney World, this is the perfect book for you! The details here will entertain and inform you and help create a more immersive Disney experience. When you visit a Disney park, or ride your favorite attractions, you'll know just a little bit more about them and the secrets and history behind what makes them so special.

Thank you for reading this book. I hope you enjoy this journey though the magic of the secrets and history of Walt Disney World.

Have a Magical Day!
Adam

CHAPTER 1 – MAGIC KINGDOM

1) There is a series of tunnels built underneath Magic Kingdom known as Utilidors. The tunnels are used so that guests in the park won't end up seeing a character from one 'land' out of place in another as they travel to and from their appropriate place in the park. For example, you'll never see a cowboy from Frontierland in Tomorrowland, or Buzz Lightyear next to Splash Mountain- this would ruin the illusion. The Utilidors are also used to elevate the park off of Florida's low water table, because tunnels could not be built underground without flooding. This means that Magic Kingdom is actually on the second level of the Park's property. As proof of this, note the elevation of Magic Kingdom (below) is 13 feet higher than the official elevation of Lake Buena Vista (95 feet), the city in which Walt Disney World is located.

Magic Kingdom: Elevation 108 ft.

2) Within Magic Kingdom's Utilidors are systems of trash chutes that shoot the garbage around the park at up to 60mph in order to keep the disposal system efficient. That paper cup that you threw away an hour ago could already be over a mile away!

Mickey & Minnie heading out for another day at the office

3) In Magic Kingdom, any guest will never be more than thirty steps away from a trash can. Before building the park, Walt Disney went to other parks and tried to figure out how long a person would carry around a piece of garbage before just dropping it on the ground and moving on. Thirty steps were what he found to be the magic number.

4) While purchasing the land for Walt Disney World, Walt Disney created fake company names such as M.T. Lott Real Estate Investments, Ayefour (a pun on

the local Interstate 4 highway), and Retlaw (Walter spelled backwards) in order to keep his Florida Project a secret. On Main Street U.S.A., some of these dummy corporation names that were used are painted on the windows of some of the shops.

5) The old Magic Kingdom parking area used to have lots named after some of the Seven Dwarfs. Only six of the seven dwarfs had lots named after them though. Doc didn't have a parking lot named after him because the designers were afraid that guests would become confused and think that "Doc" meant "Dock" as in a Ferry Dock. It would be bad for half of a family to show up at a Ferry Dock and the other half to get on the Magic Kingdom tram and show up at the Doc parking lot. However, the parking lots are now named after various Disney heroes and villains.

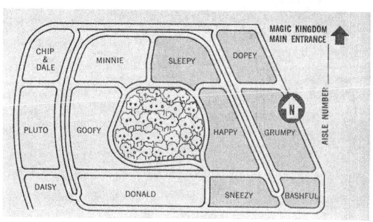

Magic Kingdom parking lots- circa 1981

6) The parking lots for Magic Kingdom are so big that they can hold the entire Disneyland park and still be able to hold 500 cars! This is because when Walt

purchased the land for his Florida Project, he wanted it to be more of an immersive experience with room for expansion- luxuries he did not have at Disneyland in Anaheim. To ensure he had this flexibility, he purchased an enormous amount of land, about 40 square miles (the size of the entire city of San Francisco) that would eventually become Walt Disney World.

7) There are two telephones in Magic Kingdom that you can pick up to hear ongoing conversations. There is one in Main Street's candy shop, and one in Tomorrowland under the Tomorrowland Transit Authority (TTA) attraction.

There is no chewing gum sold anywhere on Disney property

8) There is no gum sold in any of the Disney parks or on any of the properties at Walt Disney World. Ever notice how there is never any gum stuck to any fences or railings? Gum isn't sold anywhere at Disney because no one likes reaching under a railing and finding a wad of post-chewed nastiness stuck to their fingers.

9) A system referred to by Imagineers as "Smellitzers" is used to emit various scents throughout Magic Kingdom and the other Disney Parks. These scents are matched to specific areas of the parks. For example, On Main Street U.S.A., the Smellitzers emit scents of freshly baked pastries and coffee. You may also notice the scents of honey on The Many Adventures of Winnie the Pooh. You'll even smell the salty sea air on Pirates of the Caribbean!

10) The Haunted Mansion is a truly amazing attraction, and it has its secrets. But perhaps the most baffling of the illusions featured on the ride is the scene in the ballroom with the dancing ghosts that magically disappear and reappear right before your eyes! What many guests would predict to be a hologram is actually a simple illusion called Pepper's Ghost. Ever notice how the Doom Buggies are so high off the ground in this scene? This is because there are animatronic figures of the ghosts that you see in the ballroom dancing right below you! There is a large sheet of glass which reflects the image of the dancing ghosts to what the riders see as the ballroom. The ghosts appear to be dancing within the room itself, but what you're seeing is actually a reflection of the ghosts. That explains why all of the dancers have the

woman leading the man instead of the other way around.

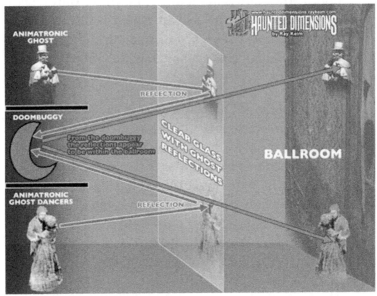

There's no such thing as ghosts... or is there?

11) In the pavement near the entrance to The Haunted Mansion there is a large ring of flat rocks sometimes referred to as the Fairy Ring. This was the location of an enormous Oak tree that was cut down during the course of the park's history. It is said that if a person stands in the ring on a night with a full moon and says, "Leota" three times, she will briefly appear in a window in the mansion holding her candle.

12) There have been three different versions of The Enchanted Tiki Room. The first version was called Tropical Serenade, but was later renamed to The Enchanted Tiki Room. Eventually, that version was replaced to The Enchanted Tiki Room (Under New

Management) and featured Lago and Zazu from the Lion King. Then in 2011, after a small fire broke out in the attraction's attic, The Enchanted Tiki room was converted back to its original format which was an edited version of the sister attraction at Disneyland in California.

A classic view of Frontierland

13) Frontierland, like Tomorrowland, was one of the original lands to make up Magic Kingdom when the park opened in 1971. However, similar to Tomorrowland, Frontierland also opened with very few attractions. It only had the railroad station, Davy Crockett's Explorer Canoes, and the Country Bear Jamboree. Over the next few decades following Frontierland's opening, Splash Mountain and Big Thunder Mountain Railroad were constructed. There was even supposed to be a boat ride themed to a western river expedition, but plans for this were scrapped when the Pirates of the Caribbean ride was

built instead to fulfill the demand for a pirate-themed ride.

14) There is an urban legend surrounding the Pirates of the Caribbean ride. It says that during the construction of the ride there was an Imagineer named George who apparently died in a possibly unrelated situation. Now, at the end of the night, the cast members who work the ride say, "Goodnight George" before turning out the lights. The legend states that the ride is haunted by George's spirit, so saying this goodbye is a way to free the ride from technical problems the next day.

BTMR: The wildest ride in the wilderness!

15) There was also another plan to build Big Thunder Mountain Railroad inside a large, plateau-themed pavilion which would house the mine train roller coaster, the western river expedition boat ride, and

many other frontier-themed rides. It would've gone where Big Thunder Mountain Railroad sits now, but it was cancelled due to the extreme costs that it would bring. So, the mine train roller coaster was built separately and some of the funds required for the plateau were transferred to the construction of Pirates of the Caribbean.

16) Big Thunder Mountain Railroad has other secrets too. A more commonly known but still sometimes unnoticed one is the names of each of the trains. On each of the locomotives, there is a nameplate which says one of six names: U.B. Bold, U.R. Daring, U.R. Courageous, I.M. Brave, I.B. Hearty and I.M. Fearless. Another uncommon fact about Big Thunder Mountain is that in the queue line, there are some crates that are labelled with, "Lytum & Hyde Explosives Company." This is one of several classic Disney wordplays that exist in Frontierland.

Magic Kingdom's Skyway

17) There used to be a Skyway ride that went from Fantasyland to Tomorrowland. It took guests back and forth from the lands in order to offer an alternative to walking. The Tomorrowland Station was demolished in 2009, ten years after the Skyway closed. The Fantasyland Station was used for stroller parking for many years, but was recently removed for a Tangled-themed meet and greet area.

18) When Magic Kingdom first opened in 1971, Tomorrowland was unfinished and not even close to being as popular as it is today. It opened with only two completed attractions, which were the Grand Prix Raceway and the Skyway. With only two attractions, many guests decided to go to other lands of Magic Kingdom because they had more to offer. In 1975, Space Mountain and The Carousel of Progress opened, which in a way put Tomorrowland on the Magic Kingdom map.

19) On the Jungle Cruise attraction over in Adventureland, in one of the scenes that the boat passes there is a group of chanting tribesman. If you listen closely, one of the tribesman is saying "I love Disco" over and over again. This is one of the many inside jokes that the attraction has to offer, along with the crates in the FastPass+ queue that are addressed to various characters at the Adventurers' Club.

20) The final cave exit before the big plunge on Splash Mountain is a Hidden Mickey. Although it is not the traditional Hidden Mickey with the three circles, it is instead a profile shape of Mickey.

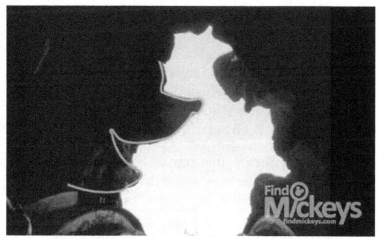

A profile hidden Mickey on Splash Mountain

21) A gopher that pops out in the cave before the final plunge yells "Go FSU!" and then goes back into his hole. This is because one of the Imagineers who worked on Splash Mountain graduated from Florida State University and decided to leave a little mark of his own on the ride.

Mr. Toad hands the deed over to Owl

22) In the Many Adventures of Winnie the Pooh, there is a picture on the wall where the riders enter Owl's house. In the picture, Mr. Toad is handing the deed of the house to Owl. This pays homage to the ride that was previously housed in this building. From 1971 to 1998, Mr. Toad's Wild Ride was in the same location occupied by Pooh today.

23) In Liberty Square, there are no bathrooms. This is keeping with the time period that the land is themed around where bathrooms weren't a thing yet. Some other thematic elements included in Liberty Square include the 13 lanterns hanging from the Liberty tree representing the 13 original colonies, and the fact that the large bell seen in Liberty Square is made from the same mold used to cast the original Liberty Bell.

24) Liberty Square has an interesting historical background. The whole area is designed to look like an American Revolution-era town square. In the area, the pavement is mostly reddish-colored concrete. However, there is a strip of brown rocky pavement that jaggedly runs through the area. This is designed to represent the raw sewage channels that ran through the streets of colonial America. Indoor plumbing was not invented yet, and as gross as it sounds, the brown pavement is supposed to be this flowing of raw sewage. Some of the other historical tidbits include two lamps in the windows of the Hall of Presidents which reference the line "One if by land, and two if by sea" written by Henry Wadsworth Longfellow. Another historical fact surrounding Liberty Square is the Presidential Seal that is on the

floor in the Hall of Presidents. This is one of only three seals installed in the country. In fact Disney had to get approval from the United States Congress in order to get the seal installed.

25) While riding it's a Small World, guests will often flick a quarter or other coin into the water that the boat attraction utilizes. Little do many people know, the coins in the water are collected and given to the organization Give Kids the World. Disney often does this with the other boat attractions it has as well.

Could this be Cinderella's horse?

26) The Prince Charming Regal Carrousel has a few secrets about it. The first secret is that the Carrousel is almost 100 years old! It will turn 100 in 2017. It wasn't always called Prince Charming's Regal Carrousel, however. Built by the Philadelphia

Toboggan Company in 1917, the original name for the ride was the Liberty Carrousel. It was originally located on Belle Isle, outside of Detroit. Later, it was rediscovered at Olympic Park in New Jersey in 1967, where Disney Imagineers bought it and refurbished it for the 1971 grand opening of Magic Kingdom.

27) Another secret about the Prince Charming Regal Carrousel is that it has one horse on it with a golden ribbon around its tail. This is rumored to be Cinderella's horse, and all other clones of the ride at other Disney parks also have this special horse. Also, a relatively unknown fact about the Carrousel is that all of the pictures around and inside of the ride are hand painted. It even has a picture of Cinderella and Prince Charming running off towards their carriage.

CHAPTER 2 – EPCOT FUTURE WORLD

28) Similar to Magic Kingdom, there is an underground tunnel at Epcot. However Epcot's tunnel is not like Magic Kingdom's in the sense that it is not a vast network of tunnels sprawling all across the park. Instead, it is simply a U-shaped pathway that goes from Innoventions West to underneath Spaceship Earth, and then to Innoventions East. The underground tunnel system at Epcot is mainly used for deliveries to the various stores and restaurants that exist in Future World.

Climb aboard Spaceship Earth

29) Florida is known for its large amounts of rain. Luckily, Disney Imagineers knew this when they were

designing Spaceship Earth because without this (very obvious) knowledge, they wouldn't have designed the gutter system on the sphere to keep all the rainwater from completely drenching everyone standing in the Spaceship Earth queue line directly beneath the ball. While it would be pretty funny to watch this happen to a queue full of people from the shelter of standing underneath an awning or something, Imagineers did not want this many people unhappy due to soaking wet socks, so they designed a complex gutter system underneath the triangular tiles that make up the outer shell of Spaceship Earth. All the rain runs off into a trough at the bottom of the ball where it then flows down the legs of the geodesic sphere and all the way to the World Showcase Lagoon.

30) Another fun fact about the Spaceship Earth attraction is that when you are on the ride, the area that seems to be the "walls" does not actually have the triangular tiles on the opposite side. The ball is made of two separate spheres, one inside of the other. The inner sphere is what actually contains the ride track and animatronics, and the outer sphere has the aluminum hubs holding the 954 triangular panels.

31) Around the backside of Spaceship Earth, there is a beautiful fountain called the Fountain of Nations. This fountain is actually incredibly powerful; it can shoot a stream of water up to 150 feet straight up into the air. This is just a mere 30 feet shorter than Spaceship Earth. This requires the fountain to pump 30,000 gallons of water per minute. Additionally, all of the water used in this fountain is cycled over and over again in what is known as a closed system.

32) The Seas with Nemo and Friends pavilion houses the world's second largest saltwater aquarium, holding 5.7 million gallons of water! This is enough to submerge the entire Spaceship Earth sphere underwater. The aquarium has many spectacular viewing areas all over the pavilion.

33) The Seas pavilion didn't always have the current Nemo and friends theming. Prior to 2005, the pavilion was known as The Living Seas, which had the backstory of taking visitors to what was known as "Sea Base Alpha". Guests would board a "hydrolator" which simulated the effects of taking an elevator underwater. In reality, the hydrolator didn't go anywhere; it simply had a shaking floor along with effects on the walls to make it look like they were going down underwater. There was also a ride called Seacabs, which was basically an omnimover ride that took riders on an underwater adventure around Sea Base Alpha. In 2001, Seacabs closed after losing its sponsorship and falling into disrepair. This began the multi-year transformation into The Seas with Nemo and Friends. In 2004, Turtle Talk with Crush was introduced, and was unexpectedly a huge success. The decision was made to fully convert the pavilion to Nemo, so the pavilion closed a year later to complete its transformation. The hydrolators and Seacabs queue were removed along with the former preshow, and the new Nemo-themed omnimover ride opened in its place.

34) There is a restaurant in The Seas with Nemo and Friends pavilion called the Coral Reef Restaurant. Naturally, the restaurant serves seafood, along with

other yummy Disney chef creations. The restaurant is unique because one of the walls is made of glass and offers a viewing area to the aquarium. The restaurant is also featured in the Full House episode entitled, "The House Meets the Mouse" where the characters in Full House travel to Disney World for a vacation. Danny Tanner and his girlfriend Vicky are eating next to the glass wall when Jesse and Joey do a radio broadcast from underwater within the aquarium.

The Coral Reef has great views of the aquarium

35) Also offered in The Seas with Nemo and Friends pavilion are the Epcot DiveQuest, the Epcot Seas Aqua Tour, and Dolphins in Depth underwater attractions. In DiveQuest, certified SCUBA divers can swim underwater in the aquarium for 40 minutes with a guided tour and free-play time. Also included is a tour of the aquarium's backstage area showing how everything works. In the Epcot Seas Aqua Tour, guests are able to swim in the aquarium with a SCUBA Assisted Snorkel (SAS), and in Dolphins in

Depth, there is a tour focused on the Seas' dolphins which ends with a waist-deep water encounter with actual dolphins.

36) The last little-known fact about The Seas with Nemo and Friends pavilion is the VIP room that the building houses. The room can be reserved for private events, weddings, or conventions, and has enormous windows with viewing to the aquarium. It even has a see through grand piano made of acrylic glass!

37) Epcot's The Land pavilion has many fan favorite attractions within its walls. It has Soarin', one of Walt Disney World's most popular attractions ever, along with Living with the Land, a relaxing boat ride through the pavilion's greenhouses. It also has Circle of Life: An Environmental Fable, which is a short film where Simba tells Timon and Pumba about the magical process known as symbiosis. Also included in the pavilion are two restaurants, Sunshine Seasons (a food court style restaurant) along with The Garden Grill, a character dining restaurant with a rotating floor and food grown within the greenhouses that the Living with the Land boats tour through. Sounds like a lot crammed into the building right? Turns out, The Land is a lot bigger than many guests initially realize. In fact, The Land covers 253,780 square feet, which was just about the size of Magic Kingdom's Fantasyland prior to its most recent expansion. The pavilion also is currently rumored to be in the process of adding a third theater to Soarin', which will make The Land even larger!

38) There is a secret meeting room atop The Land pavilion, which used to be the Kraft VIP room when they sponsored the pavilion. The room can be accessed by pushing the elevator buttons in a certain sequence. From the VIP room, the Living with the Land attraction can be seen. Kraft no longer sponsors the pavilion, so the room is now used as a training facility for new Epcot cast members. It is also used as a sort of break room for the cast members working at the Garden Grill.

The former Kraft VIP room atop The Land

39) In the safety spiel that is recited prior to boarding Soarin', the narrator Patrick Warburton (who also played Elaine's boyfriend David Puddy on Seinfeld), says that the flight you are boarding is flight number 5505. This is paying homage to the ride's opening date, May 5th, 2005.

40) Some of the audio-animatronic figures used in Living with the Land's dark ride portion originally were built under the impression that they'd eventually be in Magic Kingdom's Western River Expedition boat attraction that never opened. If the ride did open, the scenes in Living with the Land would be very different. Another interesting thing about the audio-animatronic figures is that the dog featured in the farmhouse scene is the same dog that used to be in the old Epcot attraction Horizons, in the Carousel of Progress at Magic Kingdom, and the dog that was holding the keys in its mouth from the Pirates of the Caribbean boat ride. The figure is a model of Walt Disney's dog.

Animatronic versions of Walt Disney's dog make appearances at three Disney World attractions

41) The Land Pavilion has two large murals in the walkway leading to the entrance. They were made by

a father-in-law / daughter-in-law team. In order to keep their philosophy of never making the same piece twice, on each mural on either side of the pathway there is a one tile difference. There is a ruby on one side and an emerald on the other, to represent the muralist's birthstones.

42) Living with the Land offers a behind the scenes tour called Behind the Seeds, where guests can tour the greenhouses, sample a Mickey Mouse-shaped cucumber, and even release ladybugs into the greenhouses to help the plants.

Living with the Land

43) The Imagination! Pavilion at Epcot is a less popular pavilion but it has quite an extensive history. What many visitors don't know is that there is an upstairs

to the pavilion that is somewhat of a Disney legend. The current ImageWorks exhibit was once located upstairs, but after the pavilion's 1999 refurbishment, the elements seen in ImageWorks were moved to the first floor, and the upstairs portion was left to disuse. However, in the summer of 2006, the finale of the Kim Possible interactive activity that took place all around Epcot was set up in the upstairs portion of the Imagination! pavilion. Now that the Kim Possible experience is no longer offered, the 2nd level is once again empty. Rumor says that the Rainbow tunnel that Michael Jackson once walked through is still intact though, and this leads some daring Disney treasure hunters to attempt to once again discover the 2nd floor.

44) Captain EO Tribute was originally opened in 1986. George Lucas was the executive producer of the film, which is surprising because of how terrible it is. Okay so maybe not terrible, but it is one of the corniest films ever created. It's almost a parody. Anyway, eventually Captain EO was closed and replaced with Honey, I Shrunk the Audience. This new movie stayed open for 17 years, but when Michael Jackson died, the Captain EO Tribute was put back into place. The current version still utilizes the back misters, leg ticklers, and seat shakers that Honey, I Shrunk the Audience once had.

45) Test Track is one of the most popular attractions at Epcot, but it wasn't always Test Track. Before the current Test Track ride existed, an omnimover attraction called World of Motion was in its place. The ride was themed to transportation, and featured

188 audio-animatronic figures in a total of 30 different show scenes. In 1996 the ride shut down, and Test Track opened in its place in 1999. Ever notice the wavy circular logo on the sides of the Test Track trash cans? That's the World of Motion logo, living on through both generations of Test Track rides.

The World of Motion logo can still be seen on the trash cans at Test Track

46) The SimCars that Test Track runs are the most complicated ride vehicles that Disney has produced thus far. Each car holds six people, and along with the riders onboard there is a computer which has more computing power than a space shuttle. The cars also have the capability to go 150 mph. The original

plans for the ride called for a speed that was more in the 95 mph spectrum and featured a 70 degree bank, but it was reduced to 65 mph in order to make emergency evacuations easier, because having six people hung nearly sideways on 70 degree banking would be extremely uncomfortable.

Cruising along at 65 mph on Test Track

47) Mission: Space didn't always have the Orange and Green versions of the ride. The Orange version, the more intense one, has a large spinning centrifuge which sustains a G-Force of 2.5. The Green version was introduced in 2006, and it just took one of the terminals of simulators and stopped all spinning motions. In fact, the circle in the floor which was the part that spun can still be seen in the Green simulator bay.

48) There are several references to the attraction that previously existed where Mission: Space currently resides. The attraction, called Horizons, was said to be the sequel to the Carousel of Progress in the sense

of the similar themes of the two rides. It was open from 1983-1999 and closed after it lost its corporate sponsorship, a sinkhole opened up under the building, and the roof grew nearer and nearer to collapsing under its own weight. The rotating gravity wheel in the queue line has the Horizons logo on it, which was Pac-Man-shaped and had what looked like a sun coming up over the Horizon. It is also on the cash register counter in Mission: Space's gift shop. Additionally, the planter in the front of the Mission: Space entrance is the same one left over from Horizons. The only difference is that the marquees were switched out to represent Mission: Space.

Find out if our future is in 'Jeopardy'
in Ellen's Energy Adventure

49)   The Universe of Energy pavilion only houses one ride, Ellen's Energy Adventure. However, the ride did not always feature Ellen Degeneres and her co-stars

Bill Nye the Science Guy, Alex Trebek, and Jamie Lee Curtis. Prior to 1996, the ride was simply known as Universe of Energy, and was mainly an educational show rather than the education/comedy one that it is today. In the old version of the ride, the theme song that played at the end of the ride was called "Energy, it Makes the World Go 'Round". After Ellen was added, in the movie after the dinosaur diorama the final Jeopardy song is playing, and the announcer of the show says "The winner of today's show gets a lifetime supply of energy! Energy- it makes the world go round." This is another classic example of Disney paying homage to previous attractions.

50) The moving theater cars in Ellen's Energy Adventure use similar technology to that used at Tower of Terror at Hollywood Studios to navigate around hallways while not being on a track. There is a wire in the floor that guides the cars along through the scenes that is only 1/8 of an inch thick. This seems very small compared to the weight of the cars- 30,000 lbs. when loaded!

51) Many guests have noticed the large golden dome located to the left of Mission: Space but they never knew what was in it because it is always roped off. This building is now called the Epcot Festival Center, and it is used for various events that Epcot hosts throughout the year. It was originally called Wonders of Life, and was a pavilion devoted to a theme of health and wellness. Sponsored by MetLife, Wonders of Life contained various health-oriented attractions over its 18 year history including Body Wars, the first thrill ride at Epcot.

The former Wonders of Life pavilion

When MetLife withdrew from its sponsorship in 2001, the end of the line was near for Wonders of Life. In 2004, the decision was made to operate the pavilion on a seasonal schedule only, and in 2007, Wonders of Life closed permanently. It is still used sometimes for various private events, and also during the Epcot Flower and Garden Festival held in the spring each year, and the Epcot International Food and Wine Festival held in the fall. The current state of the old Body Wars simulators is unknown, but Cranium Command, an audio-animatronic show about the brain, still exists. The theater used for a movie called The Making of Me still exists also, and is used to show various films during festivals. All signage for the attractions have been removed, however.

Epcot's Mexico pavilion

52) The Mexico pavilion is not only an impressive structure from the outside, but the inside of it is beautiful too. It features the San Angel Inn, a great Mexican restaurant, along with The Grand Fiesta Tour Starring the Three Caballeros. But a lesser known secret about the pyramid that is the Mexico pavilion is that the top of it is a launch spot for some of the Illuminations fireworks. There is a control room inside that handles various lighting effects for the show as well.

53) When the Norway pavilion first opened on May 6, 1988, it completed the World Showcase's lineup of countries. It was the most recent country added to Epcot. At the Grand Opening, Harald V of Norway (Crown Prince at the time) dedicated the pavilion and the ceremony was even broadcasted live in Norway!

54) The Chinese pavilion at Epcot features a 360-degree movie entitled "Reflections of China". The entrance to the attraction is in a re-creation of the Temple of Heaven. This building is actually acoustically perfect, which is why it echoes so well!

The Germany pavilion holds a unique secret

55) Ever notice the large building at the back of the Germany pavilion? If you knock on the wall, it turns out to be hollow. This is because of the boat ride that never opened, which would've been a ride set to a journey down the Rhine River. It was never built

because it was to be completed as part of "phase two" of Epcot, but funding was cut prior to the start of construction of the attraction. It is now used as a storage space and also as a Cast Member training facility.

56) Like Germany, the Italy pavilion had a hollow wall at the end of it that hides an attraction never built. There was supposed to be a gondola dark ride with technology similar to that of Peter Pan's Flight along with a walkthrough attraction themed to Roman Ruins, but after "phase two" was cut, the space was left empty. However, a restaurant has filled most of the space that was available, finally completing the Italy pavilion.

57) The American Adventure in the United States pavilion is truly an audio-animatronic wonder. The show features a series of scenes created by various figures that rise up from below the stage. The way Imagineers got so many audio-animatronics figures into the show is by raising the auditorium up a floor and storing all the figures below the seats on a table that has the animatronics set up by scene. The figures rise up onto the stage and lower back down as new figures are rotated into place. This explains why to get to the theater you go up the large ramp. Another interesting fact about the American Adventure pavilion is that the American Flag on display is the one that was taken from the rubble of the World Trade Center attacks on 9/11/2001.

58) Japan is yet another pavilion that has an empty building for an attraction never built. There was supposed to be a near clone of the Meet the World

attraction at Tokyo Disneyland. Meet the World is a historical narrative film covering the history of Japan. The project was dropped because the original film omits the events of World War II. Disney thought this omission might have upset veterans, so the attraction was cancelled after the show building and rotating platform were built. Other rides that were considered but never built were a simulated bullet train ride and a ride containing Godzilla.

59) The Morocco pavilion has a strong religious background. The pavilion doesn't light during Illuminations for religious reasons, and the Moroccan government even aided in the design of the pavilion in order to ensure compliance with Islamic traditions. Additionally, in accordance with Islamic religious beliefs regarding what can be included in art, none of the mosaics featured in Morocco have representations of people.

The Pont des Arts bridge in Paris from which the Epcot bridge connecting France to the UK was modeled

60) The bridge that connects the France pavilion to the United Kingdom is designed to be similar to the Pont des Arts, which is the famous bridge that spans between the Louvre museum and the Institut de France. In fact, this is the bridge where French lovers attach padlocks inscribed with their names to the railing or the grate on the side of the bridge and then throw the key into the Seine river below in a romantic gesture said to represent a couple's committed love.

61) When the United Kingdom pavilion was completed, Disney executives decided that the area looked too neat and tidy to be compared to the real thing, so ash and soot were painted on the chimneys in order to make it look more authentic.

62) Much like the China pavilion, the Canada pavilion has a 360-degree film as well, called Portraits of Canada. In 2007, the film was redone to get rid of dated Canadian stereotypes that existed in the original film made in 1979. The new film has a new host, and the original film's theme song was remade by the 2006 Canadian Idol winner Eva Avila.

63) There were two roller coaster attractions planned but never opened for World Showcase along with a number of entirely unmade pavilions. It may not seem like it, but there is room in World Showcase for around eight new pavilions. The proposed countries included Denmark, Costa Rica, Iran, Scandinavia, Russia, Israel, Spain, United Arab Emirates, Venezuela, Australia, Equatorial Africa, and Switzerland. The Switzerland pavilion was the one that was supposed to include a Matterhorn Bobsleds-type roller coaster that was themed to resemble an

undercover Swiss bobsled training facility. This sounds like a fantastic idea for a ride, but unfortunately plans fell through.

Epcot's World Showcase provides a unique perspective on architecture

64) Most of the buildings or structures in Epcot's World Showcase were built using an architectural technique called forced perspective. This is used in order to make things seem taller than they really are. For example, the large tower in the Italy pavilion is made up of bricks that get smaller and smaller as the tower gets taller. Or, the U.S.A. pavilion's American Adventure building, modeled to be just like it was built in the colonial era is actually five stories, but on the outside it only looks like three. The doors on the building are actually twelve feet tall, because in order

to go along with the architectural restrictions of the time period, the building had to be no more than three stories tall. Another example of the World Showcase's use of forced perspective is the Eiffel Tower located in the France pavilion. It gets much smaller at the top of the tower to make it seem bigger. In fact, there is a deterrent on top of the Eiffel Tower to keep birds from landing on top of it because it would ruin the effect. It would look like giant birds were taking over Paris!

CHAPTER 4 – HOLLYWOOD STUDIOS

The Hollywood Tower Hotel

65) Tower of Terror is one of the tallest buildings in all of Walt Disney World, measuring in at 199 feet. Disney has made several of their attractions 199 feet tall because if they were 200 feet then they would have to have a flashing light on top. Its pure size makes it a Hollywood Studios landmark because it is so easily seen down Sunset Boulevard. When Imagineers were designing the Hollywood Tower Hotel, they encountered a problem. The way that the new thrill ride would be positioned happened to be in alignment with the Morocco pavilion over at Epcot.

So in order to make it blend in, the paint scheme and architectural styles were chosen so that the top of the Tower of Terror wouldn't stick out like a sore thumb in Epcot. This explains why the hotel has its funny pinkish hue and its interesting spired architecture.

66) If any guests have ever watched a Twilight Zone episode, they will know Rod Serling's voice and know that it isn't the same as the one in the video that riders view in the library preshow video. Since Rod Serling died in 1975 and Tower of Terror didn't open until 1994, a different voice had to be put into place of Serling's. So voice actor Mark Silverman voiced over a clip from the Twilight Zone episode called, "It's a Good Life". Video effects specialists had to dub Silverman's voice over the clip and make it sound like it matched.

One of many 'Hidden Mickeys' at Tower of Terror

67) Tower of Terror is filled with an exceptional number of Hidden Mickeys. Disney even went as far as having the little girl in the preshow video holding a Mickey Mouse doll, and having the elevator bell above Rod Serling's head have Mickey ears. Another little nod to Mickey Mouse is in the Library room as well, but in the props. Underneath the trumpet on the desk, there is a piece of dusty sheet music entitled, "What! No Mickey Mouse?" Another instance of Mickey in the Tower of Terror is during the actual ride, when the elevator stops for the first time in the long hallway. Look up, and in the hallway's doorway there is a Hidden Mickey right in the middle.

Get ready to rock with Aerosmith

68) Rock 'n' Roller Coaster has several rock and roll references in the queue and preshow. One of the PA announcements that sometimes plays in the G-Force Records lobby mentions how there is a phone call for

Jude on line one. Then, the person on the PA says, "Hey, Jude, pick up on line one!" This is an obvious Beatles reference.

69) Some of the other PA announcements played in the Rock 'n Roller Coaster queue mention some of the Imagineers' names- paging a certain person and wanting them to report to wherever. Other references to the Imagineers that designed the attraction include names on the electrical boxes, and in the recordings playing in the studios while riders wait to enter. The recordings mention some Imagineer names, but it can be difficult to hear because it is played through a closed door.

70) Rock 'n' Roller Coaster has five trains that run on the track, although only four can be used at a time. The limo-themed trains each have a special license plate, and a specific Aerosmith song that plays during the ride. The trains say 1QKLIMO, UGOGIRL, BUHBYE, 2FAST4U, and H8TRFFC, and the Aerosmith songs played are Nine Lives, Sweet Emotion, Walk This Way, F.I.N.E., Dude (looks like a lady), and Love in an Elevator, however on the ride the line "love in an elevator" is changed to "love in a roller coaster".

71) In the back of The Magic of Disney Animation attraction, there is an empty semi-circular courtyard area with nothing but three concrete slabs in the pavement. If you look closely, the pavement is autographed by some of the original Animation Courtyard artists. It also has some pencil marks that they made, along with the date that they signed it. It is dated May 1st, 1989.

72) The Great Movie Ride's entrance is one of the only to-scale replica buildings in all of Walt Disney World. Its entrance is modeled after Grauman's Chinese Theater in Hollywood. The theater is so similar that it even includes "celebrity" handprints in the concrete out front of the building. The removal of the Sorcerer Mickey hat from Hollywood Studios has returned Hollywood Boulevard to its original look where guests see the theater down the street instead of the hat, which wasn't added until several years after the park opened.

Does the Casablanca scene feature the plane used in the movie?

73) The Casablanca scene of The Great Movie Ride where Rick is saying goodbye to Ilsa has half an airplane in it. Imagineers wanted to find the same model of airplane used in the movie, and according to urban legend, they somehow lucked out and found the exact plane used in the airport goodbye scene in Casablanca. The front half of the airplane was put in

the Great Movie Ride, and the back half is used as the crashed airplane wreckage in the Jungle Cruise over at Magic Kingdom's Adventureland.

74) The large net full of green Jell-O hanging from the ceiling in the preshow for MuppetVision 3D is one of many inside jokes and uses of visual humor that exist throughout the attraction. A net full of Jell-O is of course a play on words of Annette Funicello. Another play on words in the preshow is the display in the front of the room that says "2D Fruities" and has pictures of two-dimensional fruit.

A net full of Jell-O at Muppet Vision 3D

75) To the right of the turnstiles through which guests go at MuppetVision 3D there is a sign that mentions a key being under the mat. If someone looks under the mat, a key is actually there!

76) Streets of America has many little things that make the relatively empty area a bit more interesting. For

example, on the New York street, in some of the buildings you can hear the voices of gangsters arguing and even occasionally gunshots going off. Also, on one of the street posts there is an umbrella on the side that is like the one from "Singing in the Rain". This is not only a funny photo opportunity but a nice place to cool off. If the black tile in the cement near the street post is stepped on, above the umbrella it actually begins to "rain". Another thing that can happen is the fire hydrant in front of the New York Street hotel will occasionally squirt water at unsuspecting visitors passing by!

77) There is a hidden Kermit the frog in Star Tours! A droid shaped like Kermit (and without the green skin) is with the other droids to the right of the boarding area.

78) The Star Wars movies were directed by George Lucas, and George Lucas likes to put little mentions to himself and other references in all of his movies. Over the PA announcements, listen carefully and you may hear a droid page for Egroeg Sacul, which is George Lucas spelled backwards. You may also hear references to "THX1138" which pays homage to a 1971 science fiction film directed by Lucas. This number can be seen or heard in all of Lucas' movies.

79) Chances are, each time someone rides Star Tours they will have a different experience. There are two pre-light speed scenarios, three post-light speed scenarios, and following this for most of the show there are three additional scenarios that can happen. In total, there are 18 different random shows, and

chances are that unless you ride many, many times, you'll never see the same show twice.

George Lucas has made his mark at Hollywood Studios

80) George Lucas is heavily affiliated with Disney, especially in Hollywood Studios. In addition to teaming up with Imagineers for both versions of Star Tours (pre-renovation and current version), Lucas also worked on the development of Indiana Jones Epic Stunt Spectacular along with all other various Indiana Jones themed attractions at Disney parks around the world. He even worked on Captain EO over at Epcot.

81) Not really a "secret" per se, but an interesting piece of information regarding the Indiana Jones Epic Stunt Spectacular is located in the queue. There is a little display that has a well with a rope attached to it and a sign that says DO NOT PULL! Of course they want you to pull the rope, and if you do, the sound of someone stuck down in the well will be heard.

82) The shop called Mickey's of Hollywood has a façade modeled after Frederick's of Hollywood, the well-known lingerie store on Hollywood Boulevard. Of course Disney is a family-friendly environment so the merchandise sold at Mickey's of Hollywood is very different. You won't find anything similar in any way to anything sold at Frederick's of Hollywood at Mickey's.

Mickey's (not Fredericks) of Hollywood

83) The giant green dinosaur on Echo Lake is a reference to a very important character in the history of animation. It is a model of Gertie the Dinosaur, who was the very first animated character ever. The tagline said "Gertie: She's a scream!" So naturally, with Disney loving puns as much as they do, the Hollywood Studios Gertie the Dinosaur is an ice cream stand.

84) In Hollywood Studios' Brown Derby, the various pictures on the walls are either in a gold or black

frame. The pictures in the black frames represent the pictures that are copies of the originals, and the pictures in the gold frames are the actual pictures that were in the original Brown Derby restaurant in Hollywood, California which is no longer in existence.

86) Animal Kingdom is a lot bigger than many people realize. The park covers 500 acres of Walt Disney World property, making it the second largest theme park on the planet, behind Six Flags Great Adventure in Jackson, New Jersey. The park's largest attraction, Kilimanjaro Safaris, covers a large amount of this land for only one attraction. The safari spans over 4,791,600 square feet!

*See roaming rhinos on the savannah
at Kilimanjaro Safaris*

87) The animal conservation theme at Animal Kingdom was originally highly controversial. Various animal rights groups both nationally and locally tried protesting the construction of the park by telling people not to go there because it was bad for animals

and other things like that. They even tried convincing travel agencies not to book trips to Animal Kingdom because they thought it would prevent people from going to the park. There was even a problem on opening day of Animal Kingdom where rumors circulated that there would be a large protest, so the Orange County Sherriff's office sent in 150 deputies in case the protest was as big as it was said to be. However, only 24 people showed up so the deputies were unnecessary.

Animal Kingdom's Tree of Life

88) The icon of Animal Kingdom, the Tree of Life, is about as much alive as a bunch of steel, and it is as much a tree as an oil rig. In fact, the Tree of Life is an offshore oil rig that Disney trucked in in order to

create the park's landmark. The oil rig was turned upside down, and 100,000 fake leaves along with 7,000 branches were added to it, as well as sculpted and painted concrete in order to make it look more realistic. Over 300 different animals are carved into the Tree of Life's "bark", including a sculpted image of Greybeard, the first chimpanzee observed by scientists in the wild. Greybeard is located near the entrance to It's Tough to be a Bug.

89) Animal Kingdom has a secret entrance that most guests don't know about. While lines at the front gate seem to extend almost all the way to the tram line on busy days, the secret entrance will never have a line. It is located through the Rainforest Café's gift shop, to the left of the park's main entrance. This is a good way to be the first onto Expedition Everest in the morning before the herds of people running there are even into the park yet.

90) Ever notice the dragon on the Animal Kingdom logo? This is kind of odd considering the fact that there are no dragons in the park. Originally, in the spot where Camp Minnie-Mickey was supposed to be built was a themed land called Beastly Kingdom, themed to animals of the imaginary variety. Plans for Beastly Kingdom fell through because of budget reasons, so the cheaper space filler of Camp Minnie-Mickey was built. Other remnants of Beastly Kingdom and the imaginary category of creatures and animals include the Unicorn parking lot, and the dragonhead statue on top of a ticket booth at the park's entrance.

Another reason explaining why Beastly Kingdom was never built is because after plans for it were scrapped the first time, Universal's Islands of Adventure just a few miles away opened with both a Dragon themed roller coaster and a Unicorn themed family roller coaster, two possible concepts for Beastly Kingdom. If Animal Kingdom ever did build Beastly Kingdom, they would look like copycats. But with the Avatar Land expansion currently under construction on the spot previously occupied by Camp Minnie Mickey (Beastly Kingdom's spot), Animal kingdom is finally fulfilling the original idea of representing creatures that are extinct, real, and imaginary.

Can you spot the dragon at the Animal Kingdom entrance?

91) The cracks and unevenness of Animal Kingdom's pathways were made on purpose. The mold in the concrete was made with prints of leaves and mud already on it, and the cracks in the pavement were expanded using pressured jets of water. Additionally,

the "asphalt" around the area where the Primeval Whirl roller coaster sits is not actually asphalt; it is just treated concrete. In the Florida heat real asphalt can heat up and things can sink down into it. This is especially true for high heels, because for whatever reason it is 2015 and people STILL wear high heels into theme parks.

92) While Kilimanjaro Safaris are modeled after an African plain, the wild factor that would exist on a real African plains region is not entirely present. The various species of animals are segregated across the Safari's land, because Disney wanted to make sure that visitors on the safari still see animals and also to ensure the animals' safety. Imagineers worked hard in order to hide these barriers, so they camouflaged them in fallen trees, hidden fences, and a cleverly placed river or canyon in order to keep the animals out of each other's zones. For example, the lions are kept within their habitat by they use of cool air jets to entice the lions to not want to leave, along with an 18 foot deep, 21 foot wide moat that is hidden from safari goers' views.

93) A program called enrichment is used on Kilimanjaro Safaris in order to make each safari interesting and different. Basically, enrichment is changing an animal's environment every so often in order to keep them interested and moving. The animals are also "bribed" into being in the picture-perfect spot by hiding food troughs in fallen logs, in the side of tree branches, and in other areas that are out of the views of the people of the Safari Truck. By putting food in the places where people want the animals to be, each

safari will include several encounters with animals that are most likely closer than anyone could get at a regular zoo.

94) In the Dinosaur ride in DinoLand U.S.A., along the wall are three pipes that are red, yellow, and white. There are chemical formulas written on each of the pipes that are meant to look scientific and complicated. But these are actually the chemical formulas for Ketchup, Mustard, and Mayo. This seems really random, but McDonalds used to be the sponsor of Dinosaur so that might be the reason.

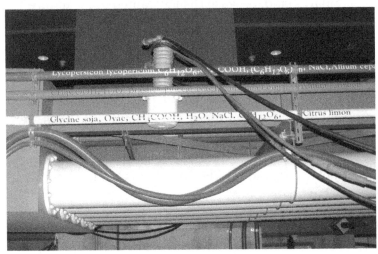

Secret formulas on Dinosaur!

95) Animal Kingdom's lush jungle hides many different plant and animal exhibits. But the plants and animals aren't the only things that are alive. Expertly camouflaged and silently graceful, the "living statue" known as DiVine walks through the trees and leaves guests in awe. But before DiVine, there was Bamboo,

a more masculine version of the same concept. Bamboo was more interactive however, as he would sometimes pose with guests for pictures. There was never an official reason as to why Bamboo was retired.

96) The Oasis Gardens section of Animal Kingdom was originally meant to be called Genesis Gardens. However, it was later renamed to Oasis Gardens because of the religious connotations of the word Genesis.

Disco Yeti is Stayin' Alive on Everest

97) Expedition Everest is known for being one of the most thrilling rides in all of Walt Disney World. Of course, the roller coaster track and trains along with the artificial mountain to house it come with a cost. Expedition Everest was built in three separate

structures, the roller coaster, the mountain, and the structure that holds the Yeti, the largest and most complex audio-animatronic figure that Imagineers have ever created. Unfortunately, the Yeti's concrete structure cracked a few months after the coaster's opening, limiting it to only operating in "B-mode", which is basically just flashing strobe lights on it to make it appear to move. This earned it the nickname "Disco Yeti". So the giant monster clawing at the riders as they race by at the end of the ride is actually just a lighting effect.

98) Another fun fact about the Yeti: while it is just an animatronic, it is still extremely powerful. The yeti has a potential thrust of just over 259,000 pounds of force if all of its hydraulic cylinders were activated simultaneously. This insane amount of thrust is more instantaneously powerful than a 747 airliner.

99) Animal Kingdom's top priority is the safety of their animals. After all, the park is dedicated to animal conservation. The park has over 1,000 animals representing more than 250 different species. Did you ever notice the weird straws and lack of lids on the drinks? The straws are paper and the cups are biodegradable in order to keep the animals safe in case a guest litters. If an animal happened to get ahold of a plastic lid or straw, it could severely sicken or even kill the animal.

100) The Highway route sign over in DinoLand U.S.A. has the signature Disney hidden meaning to it like many other Disney parks signs and artifacts. The highway sign in Diggs County in DinoLand U.S.A. says US

498, representing the month and year that Animal Kingdom opened: April of 1998.

101) On the peninsula that juts out into the wide opening of the Discovery River across from Expedition Everest, there is a pinkish-brown statue of an Indian temple. The statue is designed to have a similar shape to Expedition Everest's peaks. If lined up correctly, the outline of the mountain and the temple match each other. This is a neat sight to see and it makes a great photo opportunity.

Note the way the sculpture is the exact same shape as the mountain behind it

WAIT- There's one more thing...

I truly hope you've enjoyed this journey through the history and mysteries of Walt Disney World. The parks have certainly seen many changes over the years, and it was quite interesting for me to compile the research necessary to bring some of the excitement to you. The next time you visit Walt Disney World, I'll bet you'll see the rides, shows, and attractions in an entirely new way now that you know so many of their secrets!

Have a magical day!

If you've enjoyed this book, I hope you'll share it with family & friends. I would love it if you would **please** visit the Amazon book page to post a short review. It just takes a minute. If you scroll down the page and click the **Write a Customer Review** button it will help me share these experiences with others.

Please take a minute to "Like" our family Disney Facebook page at: www.facebook.com/DisneyVacations4Families and follow us on Twitter (@Disney4Families). With so many changes constantly occurring at Disney, it's guaranteed that something will be different a few months down the road. We'll post many park updates on Facebook and Twitter, so that's the best way to keep in touch. This is also where we'll announce new books, updates, book sales and FREE BOOK promotions. If you'd like to see some great park videos including ride POVs, please also subscribe to our YouTube channel at: www.youtube.com/user/DisneyVacations4Fams.

Thanks- and have a magical day!

The Complete Guide to FastPass+ and My Disney Experience

Don't leave home without the ONLY guide to provide complete coverage of Disney's FastPass+ reservation system AND My Disney Experience! This complete guide to every FP+ attraction with maps to FP+ kiosks will help you make the most of your Disney vacation. Get the **Complete Guide to FastPass+ and My Disney Experience** today!!!

Discover the Magic: The Ultimate Insider's Guide to Walt Disney World

The all new for 2015 Ultimate Walt Disney World theme park guide packed with vacation planning and travel tips for Magic Kingdom, Epcot, Hollywood Studios, Animal Kingdom- and even Disney's awesome water parks: Typhoon Lagoon and Blizzard Beach! Discover Disney resorts like never before. **Discover the Magic** will guide you every step of the way. **Discover the Magic** of a Disney vacation today!!!

Keys to the Kingdom: Your Complete Guide to Walt Disney World's Magic Kingdom Theme Park

Prepare to be enchanted by the **Magic Kingdom!**
In **Keys to the Kingdom** you'll find everything you need to make the most of your Disney vacation including detailed maps, ride guides, dining guides, and more! You'll also get complete guides to Magic Kingdom's awesome shows & parades supported by nearly 70 photos, maps, and charts. Get your **Keys to the Kingdom** today!

Disney Christmas Magic: The Ultimate Insider's Guide to Spending the Holidays at Walt Disney World

Experience the happiest place on Earth during the most magical season on Earth- the Christmas holiday season! Learn all about the special holiday events at Walt Disney World like Mickey's Very Merry Christmas Party, Epcot's Candlelight Processional, and the Osborne Family Spectacle of Dancing Lights! Discover Disney Christmas Magic today!!!

Disney Tips & Secrets: Unlocking the Magic of a Walt Disney World Vacation

Experience a magical Disney vacation- updated and EXPANDED with 240 tips and secrets to save time and MONEY while taking the stress out of your Disney vacation. Visit any park, or visit them all... We've got you covered! Discover hidden paths and a secret exit from The Magic Kingdom. Learn the secrets to great vacation photos! Get **Disney Tips & Secrets** today!!!